The Clever Camper Cookbook

The Clever Camper Cookbook

Over 20 simple dishes to enjoy in the great outdoors

Megan Winter-Barker and Simon Fielding

DOG 'N' BONE

www.rylandpeters.com

Published in 2018 by Dog 'n' Bone Books
An imprint of Ryland Peters & Small Ltd
20–21 Jockey's Fields   341 E 116th St
London WC1R 4BW   New York, NY 10029
www.rylandpeters.com

10 9 8 7 6 5 4 3 2 1

ISBN: 978 1 911026 41 9

Printed in China

Editor: Gillian Haslam
Design concept: Megan Winter-Barker
Additional design: Eliana Holder
Illustrator: Kate Sutton
Photography: John Winter-Barker, Paul Anderson,
Ewan Faichnie, Megan Winter-Barker, Simon Fielding,
Ann Fielding, Richard Fielding, Chris Loxton
Additonal recipe photography on pages 11 (center), 17, 21,
25 (bottom), 26, 31, 41, 54, 61 (top right, bottom left) by
photographer: Stephen Conroy; food stylist: Kim Sullivan;
home economist: Tamara Voss

Book originally created by Megan Winter-Barker as part of
the University of Central Lancashire Publishing Course.

uclanpublishing

CONTENTS

HELLO!

Just a quick hello from us, Meg and Si, the authors of *The Clever Camper Cookbook*.

We are both keen travelers and big foodies! We love to cook and we believe that even when camping you can cook up tasty and practical meals that won't cost loads when you're on a tight traveling budget.

This book began as a twinkle in our eyes on our own campervan adventures. Traveling for two months and never staying in one place for long, we became very good at cooking up tasty and interesting dishes on our little two-burner stove and finding ways to use up whatever we had left in our tiny fridge. With hardly any storage we had to find new ways to cook the meals we loved, without wasting anything!

This book is a compilation of some of our favorite recipes that we cooked while we were away. It is designed to help you maximize space, use up leftovers, and cook delicious, hearty food while traveling in your van or even just camping with family or friends.

Buy all the ingredients from the shopping list overleaf and you can cook any of the meals in the book. No fuss, no fancy ingredients, just tasty, simple cooking. You can also use the keycode to quickly and easily see the ingredients each recipe contains, to help you use up any leftovers. There's also a rough time for how long the recipe will take to cook.

All the recipes make enough for two people, but they are all really easy to increase if necessary. We have tried to give quantities in amounts you can easily measure, such as cups or handfuls, as we know you're unlikely to have a set of measuring scales in the van, but for most recipes the quantities are for guidance and can be changed to taste.

We hope you enjoy the recipes, and happy camping!

SHOPPING LIST

IN THE CUPBOARD

Stock up once on these ingredients and you should be set for at least a week's camping and cooking!

Carbs

Dried pasta
Risotto and basmati rice
Bread

Herbs, spices & flavorings

Red pepper (chili) flakes
Mixed herbs
Basil
Salt and freshly ground
    black pepper
Fajita spice mix
Stock cubes

Cans & Jars

Wholegrain mustard
Honey
14-oz (400-g) can of tomatoes
14-oz (400-g) can of beans
    (your choice of type)
Coconut milk

Condiments

Soy sauce
Sweet chili sauce
Olive oil
Basil pesto
Peanut butter
Tomato paste (purée)
Curry paste

Baking

All-purpose (plain) flour
Dried yeast sachets

Fruit & veg

Garlic
Onions
Potatoes

Sweet things

Marshmallows
Chocolate buttons
Favorite cookies (biscuits)

IN THE FRIDGE

You've probably got little, if any, fridge space, so stock up on these ingredients as and when you need to. If you're running out of room, there will always be a recipe to help you use up whatever's left!

Meat & fish

Chicken breast
Bacon
Ground (minced) beef
    (1lb 2oz/500g pack)
Chorizo ring
Salmon fillets

Dairy

Cheese (Cheddar and/or
    Parmesan are best)
Butter
Milk
Crème fraîche
    (or sour cream)
Eggs

Fresh fruit & veg

Scallions (spring onions)
Bell peppers
Mushrooms
Cherry tomatoes
Chilis
Green beans
Zucchini (courgettes)
Bananas
Strawberries
Cilantro (coriander)

USEFUL EQUIPMENT

We recommend investing in a really good-quality non-stick deep skillet (frying pan), preferably with a lid, that you can use for everything, from cooking fried breakfasts and pancakes, to pasta and one-pot dishes. The better the pan, the easier the washing up!

Here's a short list of some other items that we found really useful while we were cooking and traveling:

Regular pan with a lid, for boiling pasta, etc
Flat-pack colander (a great space-saving item)
Silicone spatulas (great for easy washing up)
Garlic crusher
Measuring spoons & cups
Measuring jug
Skewers
Two chopping boards
Knives with protective sheaths
Can opener
Bottle opener
Cheese grater
Peeler
BBQ tongs
Kettle
Lighter/matches
Kitchen foil

USING THE KEY

There is a simple key to help you easily see the main ingredients used in each recipe. This way you can flick through the book and choose dishes based on which ingredients you need to use up.

15 MINS

30 MINS

45 MINS

60+ MINS

CRÈME FRAÎCHE
EGG
CHEESE
MILK

BEEF
CHORIZO
CHICKEN
BACON
FISH

POTATO
PASTA
BREAD

TOMATO
MUSHROOM
CHILI
BELL PEPPER
BANANA

BREAKFAST

THE BEST BREAKFAST SANDWICH

Start the day right with a bacon and egg sandwich. Do you like your eggs fried or scrambled? Here's a recipe for both, but Simon's scrambled eggs are the best and are perfect for a large group—less washing up! His secret is "low and slow."

Ingredients

For 2 sandwiches:

4 slices of bacon

2 teaspoons butter

4 eggs

Splash of milk (if scrambling the eggs)

Salt and freshly ground black pepper

Soft rolls or slices of toasted bread

Ketchup or spicy sauce, to serve

Method

Place your slices of bacon on a grill pan with the grill set to medium or in a skillet (frying pan) over a medium heat and cook, turning occasionally to make sure the bacon cooks evenly.

If you're frying the eggs, add a knob of butter to a skillet (frying pan) and melt over a medium heat so the pan is coated. Crack your eggs into the pan, taking care not to break the yolks, and fry, adjusting the heat if necessary so the undersides of the eggs don't burn. If you like your yolk runny, remove the eggs once the whites have set. Otherwise, cook for a minute or two longer and remove from the pan.

For scrambled eggs, crack all the eggs into a cold pan (preferably non-stick) and add the butter and milk with a bit of salt and lots of black pepper. Start with the pan over a medium heat, then once the pan is warm turn it down to a very gentle heat. Don't whisk the eggs, just stir gently, and continue to cook the eggs slowly over a low heat. Be patient!

Personally we like our scrambled eggs a bit sloppy, but keep cooking until the eggs are nearly at the consistency you want. Take them off the heat, as they will finish cooking from the residual heat in the pan for a few minutes.

Put the bacon and eggs in a soft roll or on toast and serve with ketchup, spicy sauce, or whatever takes your fancy.

BANANA EGGY BREAD

Most days in the van we get up and go exploring or set off to a new place. But on the odd occasions when we are rained in or having a chilled-out day, this breakfast is the perfect treat. It's no hassle and a bit indulgent—a Sunday morning special in the campervan.

Ingredients

1 banana

1 egg

2 tablespoons milk

Knob of butter

Splash of olive oil, for frying

2 thick slices of bread

Honey or peanut butter, to serve (optional)

Method

In a bowl, mash the banana with a fork. Once mashed, add the egg and milk, then mix together.

Melt the butter in a non-stick skillet (frying pan) and add a splash of oil.

Take a slice of bread and place it into your banana mixture so that it's covered all over and the mixture is soaking into the bread.

Once coated, place the bread flat into your pan and cook over a medium heat for 1½ –2 minutes. Then flip it and cook on the other side for the same time, or until both sides are golden brown. Repeat with the second slice of bread.

Serve straight away with a drizzle of honey or a spoonful of peanut butter, if you like.

If you're going back for round two, just double the banana-egg mixture and then repeat the method, adding a little more butter to your pan when you cook each new batch.

Handy hint

If slicing your own bread, make sure they're thick slices. A good farmhouse white loaf is nice, but whatever bread you have will be just as tasty.

Mix it up

We've made our eggy bread sweet, adding banana and honey, but you could leave out the banana and fry some bacon to serve as an accompaniment. Try drizzling a little bit of honey on your bacon eggy bread, as the combination of saltiness and sweetness is delicious.

If you like a dose of chili heat in the morning to wake up the tastebuds, why not serve with a squirt of tangy hot sauce for a fiery savory breakfast. The amount of hot sauce you use depends on how much you think you can handle.

ONE-POT MEXICAN BREAKFAST WITH CHORIZO & POACHED EGGS

We both love spicy food, and this is a perfect start to our mornings.
It's a versatile dish that makes for a great dinner as well.

Ingredients

4-in (10-cm) piece of chorizo, sliced

½ red onion, finely chopped

1 clove of garlic, crushed

½ x 14-oz (400-g) can of chopped tomatoes

1 tablespoon tomato paste (purée)

½ x 14-oz (400-g) can of beans (your choice of beans)

1 tablespoon fajita spice mix

1 teaspoon red pepper (chili) flakes

4 eggs

Salt and freshly ground black pepper

To serve:

Crème fraîche (or sour cream)

Fresh chili, sliced

Cilantro (coriander), to garnish (optional)

Grated cheese

Crusty bread or wraps

Method

Put a pan on the heat but don't add any oil. Once hot, add the chorizo and fry until the oil starts to be released. Turn the heat down to medium and add the onion and garlic. Fry for 5 minutes or until the onion is soft.

Add the chopped tomatoes, tomato paste (purée), and the beans (juices and all), then add the spice mix and red pepper (chili) flakes, and season. Simmer for 5–10 minutes to let the flavors develop.

When you are ready to eat, make four wells in the sauce and crack the eggs straight into them. Cover with a lid and cook for 4–5 minutes, or until the eggs are cooked through.

Serve straight away with a spoonful of crème fraîche and some sliced fresh chili if you like it spicy! We also love to add a handful of fresh cilantro (coriander) and a sprinkle of grated cheese to finish.

You can eat this dish with a slice of good crusty bread, tortilla wraps (see page 29), or even just by itself.

MAIN MEALS

PASTA CARBONARA

We cook this a lot in the campervan. It's one of those comforting meals that is super-tasty, filling, and quick after a long day traveling. It's great for using up leftover cheese or eggs.

Ingredients

3–4 slices of bacon (smoked is good if you like it), cut into small squares

½ onion, finely chopped

1 clove of garlic, crushed

Handful of mushrooms, roughly chopped

1–1½ cups (200g) pasta

1 teaspoon wholegrain mustard

Freshly ground black pepper

Handful of grated cheese (Parmesan is best, but Cheddar works too)

2 heaped tablespoons crème fraîche (or sour cream)

2 eggs (optional)

Method

Boil the kettle, ready to start cooking your pasta.

Fry the bacon in a hot, non-stick pan. Once the bacon starts to turn crispy and release some fat, add the onion and garlic and stir. Add the mushrooms to the bacon and onions, then turn down the heat to low and cook until the onions and the mushrooms are soft.

In a separate pan, put your pasta on to cook, following the packet instructions. Traditionally spaghetti is used for a carbonara, but any kind of pasta will do.

Add the wholegrain mustard and a good seasoning of cracked black pepper to the pan of bacon, onion, and mushrooms.

Add the cheese to the bacon mix. Stir until the cheese has melted. It's up to you how much you use, as it depends how cheesy you want your carbonara to be. We love cheese, so a good handful always goes into ours!

Add the crème fraîche to the mix and stir in. Let the sauce cook over a low heat for 5 minutes.

Your pasta shouldn't be far off ready by now. When it's done, drain it and take the sauce off the heat. Add the pasta to the sauce and mix it well.

If using eggs, crack them straight into the carbonara and stir in quickly. This sounds tricky, but it's not! The heat from the pasta and sauce will cook the eggs without scrambling them and you will get a lovely rich and creamy sauce.

Serve straight away, with a sprinkle of black pepper.

CURRY WITH HOMEMADE NAAN BREAD

Everyone loves a curry, but on the road it's not always easy to find. The best bit about this recipe is how easy it is to make your own naan. Yep, even in a campervan you can have curry and all the trimmings!

Ingredients for curry

Olive oil, for frying

1 onion, roughly chopped

1 clove of garlic, crushed

2–3 tablespoons curry paste

2 chicken breasts, chopped into chunks (optional)

Handful of vegetables, roughly chopped (cauliflower, bell peppers, and mushrooms are all good in a curry)

½ x 14-oz (400-g) can of chopped tomatoes

½ x 14-oz (400-g) can of coconut milk

Rice, to serve (optional)

For the naan

¼ x 7-g sachet dried yeast

½ teaspoon honey

1½ tablespoons (20g) butter

1 cup (130g) all-purpose (plain) flour

Pinch of salt

1½ tablespoons crème fraîche (or sour cream)

Method for the curry

Remember to start making the naan bread (see opposite) before cooking the curry, as the dough needs time to rise.

To make the curry, add a splash of oil to a non-stick skillet (frying pan) over a medium-high heat. Add the onion to the pan and fry for 5 minutes or until soft. Add the garlic and stir.

Add your chosen curry paste to the pan and cook for a few minutes, stirring regularly. Add just a splash of water and keep cooking until the water has evaporated. You should have a thick, oniony sauce by now.

If using, add your chicken and cook for 3–5 minutes until it is sealed, then add your choice of vegetables and cook for 5 minutes. If you want to go veggie, just leave out the chicken.

Add the half can of chopped tomatoes and half a mug of water. Reduce the heat and simmer for 10–15 minutes, or until the chicken and veg are cooked.

Then add the half can of coconut milk (be sure to shake the can well before you open it as the milk will have separated). Stir through and cook for 5 minutes until it's hot. Serve with your homemade naan bread, and rice as well if you're really hungry.

Method for the naan bread

In a bowl, combine the yeast, honey, and $1/3$ cup (65ml) warm water and then leave for 5–10 minutes, or until the mixture starts to bubble.

Melt the butter in a pan on a low heat. Add the flour and a good pinch of salt to another bowl and make a well in the middle. Into the well, pour the melted butter, the crème fraîche, and the yeast mixture.

Start to mix together, gradually bringing in the flour from the sides as you go. It should start to make a soft, sticky dough. Take the dough out of the bowl and knead on a floury surface for about 5 minutes or until the dough is smooth.

Dust the bowl with flour, place the dough back into the bowl, cover with a kitchen towel, and leave somewhere warm for 90 minutes.

Once the dough has doubled in size, knead again briefly to knock out the air, then divide the mixture into three or four small balls. Roll the balls out into naan bread shapes (about ¼in/ 5mm thick). As you can see, Si uses a wine bottle as a rolling pin!

We grill our naan breads for just a few minutes on each side until bubbles start to form in the dough. Keep an eye on them as they burn quickly and you might need to pop the bubbles with a knife to stop them catching,

You can also cook them in a preheated non-stick skillet (frying pan) if you don't have a grill. Just cook for 5 minutes on each side over a high heat, or until golden brown and cooked through. Eat straight away.

STICKY SALMON & EGG FRIED RICE

On our travels, we used to cook our salmon fillets wrapped in foil on the BBQ, finishing them off straight on the heat to create a sweet sticky coating. We still cook this dish all the time now we're home, just in a pan—either way works just as well.

Ingredients

2 tablespoons sweet chili sauce

3 tablespoons soy sauce

2 salmon fillets

¾–1 cup (175g) basmati rice

Salt

Olive oil

1 onion, finely chopped

3 cloves of garlic, crushed

Thumb-sized piece of fresh ginger, grated (optional)

2–3 scallions (spring onions), finely chopped, plus extra for garnish

½ red or yellow bell pepper, cut into thin strips

½ zucchini (courgette), cut into thin strips

1 fresh red chili, deseeded and thinly sliced, plus extra for garnish

Handful of mushrooms, green beans, and/or cherry tomatoes (all optional—use what's to hand. Try strips of carrot or beansprouts for an Asian stir-fry)

2 eggs

Method

In a bowl mix the sweet chili sauce with 2 tablespoons of the soy sauce and then add your salmon fillets. Cover and leave for 10 minutes to marinate while you prepare the veg.

Boil your kettle and put the rice on to boil in a pan, following the packet instructions. Season with salt. Don't start cooking your salmon until your rice is cooked and drained. Cover and leave to one side for now.

When you are all prepped and ready to start cooking, put two skillets (frying pans) on the stove to heat and add a splash of oil to both. Once the oil is hot, put the salmon into one pan, skin-side down, and the onion into the other pan. Fry them both for 3–4 minutes.

When the onions are beginning to soften, add the crushed garlic and the ginger, if using.

Add all the veg (except cherry tomatoes, if using) and the chili to the pan with the salmon and fry for another 2–3 minutes. Flip the salmon, pour over any marinade left in the bowl, and add the cherry tomatoes, if using, to the pan. Fry for another 2–3 minutes.

While the salmon is cooking, add the cooked rice to the pan of onions and garlic to reheat. Add the remaining tablespoon of soy sauce and mix well. Once the rice is piping hot, turn off the heat.

Make a well in the rice so that you can see the base of the pan and crack the eggs into the hole. Fry for about 30 seconds in the residual heat in the pan, then mix the eggs through the rice. Divide the rice onto two plates straight away to stop the eggs from burning.

Flip your salmon one final time to get the skin extra crispy. When the fish is cooked through, place a fillet and half the veg on each plate and garnish with the reserved scallions (spring onions) and chilis.

The salmon is also really tasty served with noodles or potato salad (see page 55).

WHATEVER'S IN THE FRIDGE RISOTTO

Risotto is perfect for using up odds and ends in the fridge. This recipe makes a basic tasty risotto, allowing you to add your own twist using whatever ingredients are available.

Ingredients

Olive oil

1 onion, finely chopped

1 clove garlic, crushed

2 cups (500ml) chicken or vegetable stock (made with 1 stock cube)

1 cup (175g) risotto rice

Your choice of cheese, butter, or crème fraîche (or sour cream)

Salt and freshly ground black pepper

Mix it up

Make fish risotto by cooking a salmon fillet separately, then flake it and add to the risotto when you put in your creamy ingredients.

For Spanish-inspired risotto, add a chicken breast, 4in/10cm of chorizo, a bell pepper, and tomato, all chopped.

For a summery dish, add a handful of green veg with some basil pesto, and maybe 1–2 chopped slices of bacon.

Method

Heat a splash of oil in a non-stick pan, over a medium-high heat. Add the onion and fry for 2–3 minutes. (If you're using chorizo and bacon, add them now and fry until crispy.)

Next add the crushed garlic. If you're using other meat, such as chicken, add it now and fry until the meat is sealed.

Add any veg that needs a bit of time to cook, such as bell peppers, zucchini (courgettes), leeks, or mushrooms. Fry the veg for 5 minutes, then add the risotto rice. Here you can also add a splash of white or red wine, or a good tablespoon of pesto. Fry for another 2–3 minutes.

Add the stock to the pan and season to taste. Give it a stir and then turn the heat down to a simmer. It should take around 30 minutes for the rice to cook, but keep checking on your risotto, stirring regularly, and add a splash more stock or water if it starts to look dry.

When the rice is very nearly cooked, add any veg that needs a short time to cook, such as cherry tomatoes or peas, and any ingredients to make your risotto creamy. These could be a handful of grated cheese, a tablespoon of crème fraîche, or a splash of cream. Taste and season.

Cook for another 5 minutes until the rice is cooked and then serve.

FAJITAS WITH SALSA & HOMEMADE WRAPS

This is a great dish when you're starving and need food on the table quickly. Here we've gone for a traditional filling, but you can add whatever you like to your wraps and use up leftovers. Try frying some chorizo for a bit of extra spice or throw in a few cherry tomatoes for some sweetness.

Ingredients for fajitas

Olive oil

2 chicken breasts (optional), cut into thin strips

1 onion, cut into strips

1 clove of garlic, crushed

1 bell pepper, cut into strips

½ zucchini (courgette), cut into strips

1–2 tablespoons fajita spice mix

½ x 14-oz (400-g) can of mixed beans, drained (optional)

Crème fraîche (or sour cream), grated cheese (optional), and scallions (spring onions), to serve

Cilantro (coriander) and fresh red chili, to garnish (optional)

For the wraps

1 scant cup (110g) all-purpose (plain) flour

Pinch of salt

4½ tablespoons (65ml) water

Method

Heat a splash of oil in a non-stick skillet (frying pan) over a medium-high heat. Add the chicken, if using, to the pan. Stir regularly so the meat doesn't catch and cook until sealed.

Once the chicken is sealed, add the onion and the garlic and fry for 5 minutes to soften. Once soft, add the pepper and zucchini (courgette).

Cook for another 5 minutes and then add the fajita spice mix to the pan. Stir so it coats all the chicken and veg. If you're going veggie, you could add half a can of mixed beans at this point to bulk up the dish.

Cook for a few more minutes until the chicken is definitely cooked through and the spices have turned sticky and delicious.

Serve on wraps (see opposite) with a good helping of your homemade salsa (see page 30), a dollop of crème fraîche, a sprinkle of sliced scallions (spring onions), sliced chilis, and a few cilantro (coriander) leaves. Finish with a grating of cheese if you're feeling extra hungry.

Wraps

It's super easy to make your own tortilla wraps and you won't have any leftover, but you can always buy a pack of ready-made wraps and use any leftovers with our Mexican breakfast recipe on page 16.

In a bowl, mix the flour with a pinch of salt and the water. Knead for a few minutes until it forms a dough.

Divide the dough into four equal balls, then roll them out on a floury surface until they are nice and thin.

Cook them one by one in a dry non-stick pan for 1 minute on each side, or until you see bubbles starting to form.

Fill them and eat them straight away so they stay nice and soft.

Handy hint

There's no need to take up valuable storage space with a rolling pin. Just dust a wine or beer bottle (or any round bottle) with some flour and start rolling—it works just as well!

For the salsa

5 tomatoes (or 25 cherry ones)

½ red onion

1 tablespoon olive oil

2 tablespoons balsamic vinegar

Salt and freshly ground black pepper

Cilantro (coriander) and fresh chilis, chopped (optional)

Method for the salsa

To make a beautiful, fresh, tangy salsa to go with your wraps, finely chop some tomatoes (cherry tomatoes will taste just as good as large ones) and the onion (a red onion if you have it, but a white one will do too).

Put into a small bowl with the olive oil and balsamic vinegar. Season well with salt and pepper and mix together.

Keep tasting and adding more oil/ balsamic/salt and pepper until you're happy with the taste.

To liven it up, you could add fresh cilantro (coriander) or even some fresh, finely chopped chilis.

Leftovers?

Any leftover fajita filling can be saved and turned into a delicious pasta dish for the next day. Just reheat the mix in a large pan and add a few heaped tablespoons of crème fraîche. Heat gently until it creates a lovely creamy sauce. Then just add some cooked pasta and sprinkle with grated cheese to serve.

PASTA BOLOGNESE & CHILI CON CARNE

A classic bolognese never fails to please, plus it's fast and
easy to turn any leftovers into a spicy chili for the next night.

Ingredients

1lb 2oz (500g) ground (minced) beef

1 onion, finely chopped

1 clove of garlic, crushed

1 bell pepper, finely chopped

Handful of mushrooms, chopped

14-oz (400-g) can of chopped tomatoes

2 tablespoons tomato paste (purée)

1 tablespoon mixed dried herbs

2 tablespoons balsamic vinegar

Salt and freshly ground black pepper

1½–2 cups (200g) pasta

Grated cheese, to serve

To make into chili

14-oz (400-g) can of beans (kidney beans, or your choice)

1–2 tablespoons fajita spice mix

1 teaspoon red pepper (chili) flakes

1 fresh red chili, deseeded and finely chopped

Crème fraîche (or sour cream) and grated cheese, to serve

Method

Add the beef to a non-stick pan and fry over a medium-high heat until brown, breaking up the meat into small pieces.

Add the onion and the garlic and fry for a few more minutes, then add the pepper and mushrooms.

Fry for about 5 minutes or until the veg is soft, then add the chopped tomatoes and tomato paste (purée). Add the mixed herbs and balsamic vinegar, season to taste, and stir well.

Turn down the heat to a simmer, and cook for at least 30 minutes with a lid on. The longer you leave it, the tastier it will be! Keep stirring occasionally to stop it from sticking and burning.

While you're waiting, boil the kettle and cook your pasta in a pan of water, following the packet instructions.

When you're ready to eat, serve over pasta with a good handful of grated cheese sprinkled on top.

Chili for the next day

The bolognese recipe should make enough for you to turn the leftovers into a delicious spicy chili for the next day.

All you need to do is heat up the leftover mixture in your non-stick pan. Add one can of beans (kidney beans are traditional, but any can of beans will work) and the fajita spice mix. Add the teaspoon of red pepper (chili) flakes (or more if you like spice!) and the diced red chili.

Cook for about 10–15 minutes to let all the new flavors develop. Serve on a bed of rice, topped with crème fraîche and a handful of grated cheese. Or it's also great in wraps with salsa (see pages 29–30).

MEATBALLS WITH TOMATO SAUCE (PLUS BURGERS FOR ANOTHER DAY)

Cooking for two can leave you with leftover ingredients, especially if you don't want to eat the same meal every night! With these recipes you can use one packet of meat to create two meals. If there's more than two of you, just use up all the meat for the one recipe and double up on the sauce.

Ingredients for the meatballs and burgers

1 onion, finely chopped
1lb 2oz (500g) ground (minced) beef
1 clove of garlic, crushed
1 egg
All-purpose (plain) flour (optional)
Salt and freshly ground black pepper
Olive oil, for frying
1½–2 cups (200g) pasta, to serve
Handful of grated cheese, to serve

For the tomato sauce

1 clove of garlic, crushed
14-oz (400-g) can of chopped tomatoes
1 tablespoon tomato paste (purée)
1 tablespoon mixed dried herbs
Splash of balsamic vinegar
1 teaspoon sugar (optional)
Red wine (optional)

Method

Heat a splash of oil in a non-stick pan. When hot, add the onion and fry until soft and translucent.

When cooked, turn off the heat and remove half of the onions from the pan, place in a large mixing bowl and allow to cool. Leave the rest in the pan— you'll use these later to make your tomato sauce.

Once the onions in the bowl have cooled, add the beef and garlic. Add the egg to bind the mixture and mix well using your hands. If the mix is too loose, gradually add plain flour until you're happy with the consistency.

Now choose your flavor! You can cook the mixture as it is (just season well with salt and pepper), or get a bit creative. You'll use half the meat for your meatballs and half for your burgers for another day, so if you want to flavor them differently (see page 39 for ideas), split the mixture in half at this point.

Once mixed, shape the meat into meatballs and burgers. For meatballs, form the mixture into ping-pong sized balls (roughly 3–4 per person) and squeeze them gently to help them keep their shape. For burgers, gently flatten the mixture to make sure they don't fall apart when you cook them.

If possible, put the meatballs/burgers in the fridge for 30–60 minutes to set.

Method for tomato sauce

With the meatballs, we like to make a traditional tomato sauce and serve with pasta for a hearty meal.

Remember those onions still in the pan? Place them back over a low heat and add the crushed garlic.

Next, add the chopped tomatoes, tomato paste (purée), mixed herbs, a splash of balsamic vinegar, and the sugar (if you have it). If you have any, you can add some leftover grated cheese too—just a little chunk to add some flavor. If, like us, you happen to enjoy a glass of red wine with dinner, add a little splash to your sauce to give it a beautifully rich flavor. Season with salt and pepper to taste.

Turn up the heat and cook for 5 minutes to reduce the sauce slightly, then simmer away until you are ready to add the sauce to your meatballs (see overleaf).

Cooking the meatballs

In a separate pan heat a splash of oil.

When hot, add your meatballs from the fridge and seal on all sides, moving them around carefully so they don't break or stick to the pan.

When they're brown all over, add the tomato sauce (see page 37) to the pan with the meatballs to get all the meaty flavor from the pan into your sauce. Add a splash of water if the sauce is a bit thick. Cover and simmer for about 20 minutes. Try not to stir it too much—you've got to treat the meatballs gently!

Boil your kettle and cook your pasta in a pan following the packet instructions. Once your pasta is done, the meatballs should be cooked through (cut one in half to check).

Drain your pasta and dish out the meatballs with a generous helping of tomato sauce. Top with grated cheese if you like.

Cooking the burgers

You can either fry your burgers in a skillet (frying pan) or stick them on the BBQ. They'll need to cook for about 10–15 minutes or until they are cooked to your liking. Just keep gently turning them every couple of minutes so they don't catch on one side. Depending on your flavoring, you can serve them the good old-fashioned way in a nice fresh bun and the condiments of your choice, or they also go perfectly with our potato salad for a summer BBQ-style meal (see page 55).

Variations

For more options, here are a few recipe tweaks you can try.

Spanish meatballs

Add some diced cooked chorizo to your mix and a teaspoon of smoked paprika, then serve with fried cubes of potatoes and a tomato sauce (see recipe on page 37), patatas bravas style.

Italian-style burgers or meatballs

Add some leftover grated cheese to your meat and a splash of balsamic vinegar. Stir in with a tablespoon of tomato paste (purée) and a teaspoon of mixed herbs.

Mexican burgers

Add 1 teaspoon of fajita spice to your meat before cooking, and serve with fresh tomato salsa (see page 30) and cilantro (coriander).

These are just some suggestions, but you can add whatever you fancy to flavor your burgers. In the past we've used pesto, sundried tomatoes, olives—it's a great way to use up odds and ends in the fridge. Just make sure you chop everything really small and combine it well into the mixture. It's best just to get in there and use your hands.

SATAY CHICKEN

This recipe is something a little different to cook while camping.
The Thai-style satay sauce is really easy to make and you can make
a veggie version by replacing the meat with more vegetables.

Ingredients

2 heaped tablespoons peanut butter

½ x 14-oz (400-g) can of coconut milk

2 tablespoons sweet chili sauce

2 tablespoons soy sauce

1 cup (200g) rice

Olive oil

½ onion, roughly chopped

2 chicken breasts, cut into large chunks

1 clove of garlic, crushed

1 bell pepper (a variety of colors is nice, but half a pepper per person will do), chopped

Salt and freshly ground black pepper

1 fresh chili, chopped, to serve

1 tablespoon freshly chopped cilantro (coriander), to serve

Method

Place the peanut butter and coconut milk in a non-stick saucepan over a low heat. Keep stirring the mixture until the peanut butter has melted. Be careful not to burn it! Once melted, add the sweet chili and soy sauces to the mixture, stir, then take off the heat and transfer the sauce to a bowl. Wipe out the pan.

Put your saucepan back on a medium-high heat and add a splash of oil. Add the onion to the pan and cook for 5 minutes until soft. Then add the chicken and the garlic to the onions. Keep stirring so it doesn't catch and cook over a high heat until the chicken has browned on all sides. Then add the pepper.

Boil your kettle and cook the rice according to the packet instructions.

Add the satay sauce you made earlier to the chicken and veg and turn the heat right down. Season to taste. Cook the mixture with a lid on for 10–15 minutes, or until the chicken is cooked all the way through. By the time the rice is cooked, the chicken should be ready.

Drain the rice and season the satay sauce to taste. Serve on a bed of rice (or noodles are good too) and garnish with fresh chili and cilantro (coriander).

Mix it up

If you like extra spice, add some chopped fresh red chili or red pepper (chili) flakes to the sauce when you add the garlic. You could also add some thinly sliced scallions (spring onions) as a garnish, plus some chopped peanuts or cashew nuts that have been lightly toasted in a dry pan.

ONE-POT SPICY CHORIZO & BEAN STEW

This spicy, rich dish is perfect on chilly nights when you need warming up. It's also great for feeding lots of people—just bulk up on potatoes or butternut squash or even BBQ some sausages and throw them in at the end for a hearty meal. We like to eat it with a good chunk of fresh bread, but you could also serve it with rice.

Ingredients

4–5in (10–15cm) piece of chorizo (approx 3oz/75g), sliced

½ onion, chopped

1 clove of garlic, crushed

1–2 potatoes or sweet potatoes, or ¼ butternut squash, peeled and cut into small chunks (optional)

14-oz (400-g) can of chopped tomatoes

2 tablespoons tomato paste (purée)

2 tablespoons balsamic vinegar

1 tablespoon fajita spice mix

1 teaspoon red pepper (chili) flakes (optional)

14-oz (400-g) can of beans (mixed beans, kidney beans, or whatever you fancy will do)

Fresh crusty bread and a good spoonful of crème fraîche (or sour cream), to serve

A few cilantro (coriander) leaves, to garnish

Method

In a large hot pan, fry the slices of chorizo until they start to release their oil. Add the onion and the garlic to the pan and stir to make sure they don't catch. At this stage, if you wish, you can add potato, sweet potato, or butternut squash to bulk the dish out a bit. If you're short of time, parboil the veg first.

Fry the mixture for 3–5 minutes until the onion (and the potato or squash) is turning brown.

Add the chopped tomatoes and tomato paste (purée). Turn the heat down to a simmer. You might need to add some water to loosen the sauce—just half-fill the empty chopped tomato can and that should do it.

Add the balsamic vinegar and the fajita spice mix to the pan. If you like it spicy, you can also add a teaspoon of red pepper (chili) flakes.

Cover and simmer for 40 minutes to bring out all the spices and flavors, or until the potato (if using) is soft and breaks apart on a fork. Keep checking and stirring, adding more water if necessary to stop the mixture catching.

Add the tin of beans, juices and all, and season to taste. Turn the heat back up and cook until it is hot. Serve in bowls with chunks of bread and some crème fraîche to cool down those spices, and scatter over a few cilantro (coriander) leaves.

Mix it up

Bean stews are a mainstay in our campervan because they are so versatile. Often we'll put together an Italian version, which uses celery, carrots, and mushrooms in place of the chorizo and potato. Throw in some mixed herbs during the cooking and you're good to go.

Another easy twist is our take on the French classic, cassoulet. We fry up some bacon and sausages and add them to the tomato, garlic, and bean stew, along with some mixed herbs. We then make chunky breadcrumbs using leftover bread from breakfast to add at the end.

HANDY LEFTOVER PASTA DISHES: SPICY BALSAMIC PASTA SAUCE

Pasta dishes are great for using leftovers and creating tasty, versatile meals. The following two are just a couple of examples we like to cook. Eat them warm or take them on a picnic as a cold pasta salad.

This balsamic sauce is great with pasta, but it's also good served as a sauce for chicken breasts. Choose whatever veg you like to bulk it up and make changes, such as swapping chorizo for bacon or adding sun-dried tomatoes or a handful of olives.

Ingredients

1½–2 cups (200g) pasta

2–4in (5–10cm) chorizo, sliced

½ onion, finely chopped

1 clove of garlic, crushed

Handful of whatever veg you fancy—such as mushrooms, bell peppers, cherry tomatoes, roughly chopped

1 fresh red chili, chopped, or 1 teaspoon red pepper (chili) flakes (optional)

3 tablespoons balsamic vinegar

14-oz (400-g) can of chopped tomatoes

Salt and freshly ground black pepper

Grated cheese, to serve

Method

Boil your kettle for the pasta, then put the pasta on to cook according to the packet instructions.

Put a non-stick skillet (frying pan) on a medium-high heat. Add the sliced chorizo and fry until the oil starts to be released.

Add the onion to the pan and fry until it is soft. Add the crushed garlic and the chopped veg, plus the fresh chili or red pepper (chili) flakes, if you like it spicy.

Add the balsamic vinegar to the pan and cook it over a high heat until it has reduced down by about half.

Add the chopped tomatoes and turn down the heat to a simmer. Cook for 5 minutes or until the sauce is hot. Season to taste.

Serve over the drained pasta with some grated cheese scattered over.

HANDY LEFTOVER PASTA DISHES: ONE-POT PESTO & POTATO PASTA

This dish is inspired by an Italian classic. We've used potatoes, green beans, and tomatoes here, but any summery green veg, such as asparagus, zucchini (courgettes), or broccoli will work with the pesto. If you prefer not to boil your veg, just cook it separately and add to the pasta at the end.

Ingredients

1½–2 cups (200g) pasta

Handful of potatoes, cut into bite-sized chunks

Handful of green beans, or your choice of summery green veg, chopped if necessary

1–2 tablespoons basil pesto

Handful of cherry tomatoes, halved

Freshly ground black pepper

Grated cheese

Method

Boil your kettle for the pasta, then put the pasta on to cook in a large pan, according to the packet instructions. Add the chopped potatoes to the pan too.

Next, add your chosen vegetables to the pan. How long you cook the veg will depend on what you've chosen to use. Green beans, broccoli, and asparagus will all be done in 5 minutes, so add 5 minutes before the pasta is ready.

Check the pasta is cooked and the vegetables are tender, then drain.

Return the pasta and veg to the pan and add the basil pesto and a handful of halved cherry tomatoes.

Mix well and serve. Finish the dish with a sprinkle of black pepper and grated cheese.

ON THE SIDE

SALAD & BBQ STUFF

A barbecue is the ultimate camping meal. Here are a few easy recipes to make your lunch or dinner really special and to inspire you to up your grilling game.

Waste not, want not dressing

This dressing is the ultimate waste not, want not recipe. Once you've used up a pot of pesto, add some olive oil and balsamic vinegar to the jar. Make as much or as little as you want, sticking to the ratio of 3 parts oil to 1 part vinegar.

Put the lid on and give it a good shake to mix in any leftover pesto. Taste and add more oil or vinegar as you like.

You could also add a splash of lemon juice to the jar for a fresh citrus kick. Or add a crushed clove of garlic and a sprinkle of pepper.

The great thing about this dressing is you can keep it in the fridge for as long as you like without it spilling while you travel around. Just screw the lid back on when you're done and go!

Asian-style corn on the cob

To make the ultimate corn on the cob, try spreading the satay sauce from page 40 on your corn once it has been cooked. Then finish the corn on the BBQ to turn the sauce into a crispy, Asian-style marinade.

Croutons

Making croutons is a great way to add a bit of texture to your salad, at the same time as using up any old bread.

Chop your bread into small cubes. Heat a splash of oil in a non-stick pan over a medium-high heat, then add the bread.

Cook for 5–10 minutes or until the bread is golden brown on all sides, then remove from the pan. The croutons will crisp as they cool.

You can keep it simple, or add some flavors to your croutons. Fresh rosemary always goes well, as does a crushed clove of garlic and lots of salt and pepper.

BBQ marinade

This simple marinade will add a twist to your classic BBQ, and it's so easy to make.

All you need to do is mix your leftover curry paste from page 22 with some crème fraîche. You can use a little or a lot of paste, depending on how spicy you like it.

Then just cover your meat with the sauce and leave for an hour or two. Chicken wings or legs work well, and lamb chops or burgers can also be spiced up this way.

When ready to cook your meat, the marinade will turn into a spicy, crispy coating.

POTATO SALAD

Potato salad is the perfect addition to any BBQ, served on the side of burgers or with marinated meats and fish. It also keeps really well in the fridge. The honey gives it a lovely sweetness, while the mustard cuts through with a little tangy kick.

Ingredients

4–5 new potatoes per person (or 1–2 regular potatoes), chopped into bite-sized pieces

1 egg

2 tablespoons crème fraîche (or sour cream)

1 teaspoon honey

1 teaspoon wholegrain mustard

½ red onion or a few scallions (spring onions), diced

Method

Put your potatoes on to boil in a pan of water. After about 15 minutes add the egg to the pan and cook for another 5 minutes.

When the potatoes are cooked, drain the pan. Peel the egg and chop into small chunks.

In a bowl, mix your potatoes and chopped egg with the crème fraîche, honey and wholegrain mustard. Add the red onion or scallions (spring onions) and mix well.

Serve warm or cold.

Mix it up

If you've run out of crème fraîche, you could add a few dollops of mayonnaise instead. Some diced gherkins will go very nicely with this variation too.

Something Sweet

MARSHMALLOW & CHOCOLATE BANANAS

You can't have a BBQ without some deliciously gooey toasted marshmallows. They are even better if they come with sweet banana and melted chocolate!

Ingredients

2 bananas

1 packet of marshmallows

1 packet of chocolate buttons

Method

With the peel still on, slice your bananas open lengthways, leaving an inch (2.5cm) or so at each end unsliced. Stuff your bananas with as much chocolate and as many marshmallows as you can! Wrap the stuffed bananas separately in foil and place on the BBQ or the embers of a fire.

Leave for as long as you can before you give in and eat them. A good 20 minutes will make sure all the chocolate has melted and the marshmallows have become gooey. Unwrap, peel, and enjoy!

S'MORES

This camp-fire classic is another great way to indulge in delicious toasted marshmallows. Go on, you know you want to!

Ingredients

1 packet of marshmallows

1 packet of graham crackers (digestive biscuits)

2 bananas (optional)

1 packet of chocolate buttons (optional)

Method

This is such an easy one. Simply toast your marshmallows in the fire until lightly charred and gooey, then sandwich between two graham crackers/ digestives and devour.

You could add some sliced banana or chocolate to your sandwich as well if you're feeling fancy.

ROCKY ROAD BARS

No baking, no fuss, these are the perfect campervan treats for picnics or refueling on long walks. Don't worry about measuring ingredients precisely—rough amounts will work just fine!

Ingredients

3½oz (100g) your favorite cookies (biscuits)

5 tablespoons (70g) butter

3½oz (100g) chocolate buttons

2 tablespoons honey

3½oz (100g) marshmallows, chopped into small pieces

Method

Place your cookies (biscuits) in a sandwich bag or wrap in a clean kitchen towel and bash up into different sizes, from dust to small chunks.

Melt the butter in a pan with the chocolate and the honey over a low heat.

Take the pan off the heat and add the broken cookies and the marshmallows and mix together well. You could also add nuts, dried fruit, or even popcorn to your rocky road bars at this point.

Tip the mixture into a foil-lined tin or plastic container—anything that you can put in the fridge. Squash the mixture down so it will stick together when it sets.

Place in the fridge for at least 2 hours. When it has set, cut into squares and tuck in. Enjoy!

Mix it up

Try substituting 2 tablespoons of peanut butter for 2 tablespoons of the butter to make your bars extra moreish!

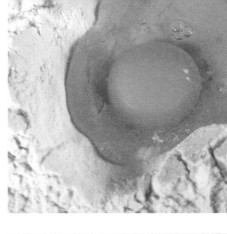

FRUIT PANCAKES

This basic crêpe recipe is so versatile—you can use it for a sweet treat, topping your pancakes with our fruity summer sauce, or for a savory dish add cheese and pieces of fried bacon, or even our chili recipe on page 33.

Ingredients

2 tablespoons butter, plus extra for cooking

1 cup (130g) all-purpose (plain) flour

2 eggs

½ cup (115ml) milk

½ cup (115ml) water

Pinch of salt

Splash of olive oil

For the sauce

1 cup (150g) strawberries, quartered, plus extra to serve

1 cup (150g) blueberries (or any of your favorite fruits), plus extra to serve

2 tablespoons honey

Method

If serving the summery sauce to top your pancakes, make it first. Add the strawberries and blueberries to a pan with the honey. Stir over a low heat for 5 minutes until you have a syrupy sauce to pour over your pancakes.

To make the batter, melt the butter in a pan over a low heat.

In a bowl whisk together the flour and eggs. Gradually add the milk and water whilst stirring. Then add the melted butter and a pinch of salt.

Heat a small knob of butter with a little splash of oil in a non-stick pan. Then, on a medium-high heat add a good spoonful of your pancake batter.

Tilt the pan around so that the batter covers the whole pan in a thin layer. Cook until the pancake is turning golden (usually 1–2 minutes on each side), flipping it halfway, or tossing if you're brave!

Serve straight away, with the sauce poured over and dotted with the extra fruit. This quantity of batter will make about 6–8 pancakes.

INDEX

ACKNOWLEDGMENTS

I've only been able to create this book with a massive amount of support and help from friends and family. It really has been a huge collaborative effort, and I've been lucky to work with so many talented people.So... to everyone who helped taste recipes, to the Andersons, especially Paul, and to everyone who came on early morning, freezing cold photoshoots, especially Ewan. To all of the Fieldings, especially Ann and Dave for letting me use Dolly the van and their house for photoshoots. To Sally, John, and Sam for their continuing belief and support, and lastly to Si, my co-author and traveling buddy, for the massive amounts of help and support you have given me throughout the project—this book would not have been possible without you.

Thank you!
Meg